2 OUTSPOKEN

TRUE COLOURS

Copyright © 2025: True Colours

All rights reserved. No part of this publication may be produced, distributed, or transmitted in any form or by any means, including photocopying, recording, or other electronic or mechanical methods, without the prior written permission of the publisher, except in the case of brief quotations embodied in critical reviews and certain other non-commercial uses permitted by copyright law.

I have tried to recreate events, locales and conversations from my memories of them. In order to maintain their anonymity in some instances I have changed the names of individuals and places, I may have changed some identifying characteristics and details such as physical properties, occupations and places of residence.

Published by Conscious Dreams Publishing
www.consciousdreamspublishing.com

Book Consultant and Editor: Daniella Blechner
Typeset and E-book formatting: Amit Dey
Cover Design: Xee_designs1

ISBN: 978-1-917584-44-9

This book is dedicated to all those
who seek justice and peace.

CONTENTS

1	Cus You're **Black**
7	No Hard Feelings
9	Sleep Less
11	Complexion Complexities (I can see)
19	i Write
21	Toxic Home
27	The Phone and its Fiends
33	Herself
35	In <u>Law</u>
41	**Class**
43	**Inger-land**
49	Bricks and Mortar
51	White Wall of **Silence**
53	Knife Down
61	Get Out

67 Waterfall
71 **Just Deserts**
75 **Not the Right Time**
79 Diss Cussers
81 The **People** Part 1
83 The **People** part 2
87 Shh the Footy's On
89 Cash Point
93 **Different**
95 Jobsworth
99 Nah **Man**
101 These **People Hate**
109 Music
115 That **Stare**
117 2 **Outspoken**
123 About the **man** himself
125 About True Colours
127 Special Thanks

CUS *YOU'RE BLACK*

"he only listens to you because you're **big** and **black**
Jeez, look at the muscles on **your** back
it's cus **you're black**
it shows **your** muscle tone more
I bet **your d@#k** drops down to the floor
no offence mate but **you** are a **big black lad**
I'm not going anywhere near her after **you've** had that
I never said that cus **you're black**
but
why do **you guys** do that?
thought I'd ask **you** cus I know **you** know that
and **you're** the first **one** not getting defensive,
at last!!
you can't say anything nowadays
I remember the days when **they** knew **their** place
now **they** get in your face if you say what you're thinking
I'm not **racist** if that's what **you're**
thinking
 sorry mate I was drinking
I don't usually say things like that

I don't want **you** to think I said it……
cus….**you're black!!**
I'd say that to any **lad**
I've got a mate like **you**
and **he** don't mind all that
he's not arsed and **he's black**
well, **he's** not **black black, he's coloured**
he does look a bit like **you brother**
jeez that got deep
are **you Muslim**? Do **you** eat meat?
cus I was watching this documentary
and this **Muslim** on it, **he** ate plenty
I'm not being funny right……
but I tell **you** who **you look** like
that **big black guy** off 'White Chicks'
you know the one who liked **white chicks**
mate don't be a dick
he looks nothing like **him**
he looks more like **Ant Joshua**
you're a **big** strapping **lad**
I bet **you've** got a right whack on **ya**
no offence mate but do you date white girls?
or just **black**?
I'm just curious and that
your tat looks class
usually, **you** can't see tats on **blacks**
nah!!!! I didn't mean it like that!!!!

I never said it cus **you're black**
but **you're** not really **black** are **ya**?
you're Jamaican aren't **ya**
you're not mad at me are **ya**?
you're a niche cus **you**'re a smart good-looking **black lad**
in fact, scratch that
you're as smooth as **Denzel**
it's mental how much **you** look and act like **him**
as well
oh yea **he** does dun **he** f'@$%&*g hell
as a matter of fact mate
is it ok if I have a pic as well mate?
I'll be dead quick mate
just want to show my mates
chilling with the Derby **Denzel** all day
excuse me mate is **your** name **Rakeem**?"
"no mate that's not me"
"**he** used to play footy for **that** team"
"oh, I see"
"well, **you** must know **who** I mean
he used to play footy for **that black** team
I lived in London with this **coloured lad** and **he** used
to call me **n%$£!***
so, I would call it **him** back
and **he** didn't mind that
we'd have a right laugh
I bet you're just like that

and **you don't sound black**
I'm sorry I hope I've not offended you
I bet **you** think I'm a right twat
you just look like a **friendly, cool dude**
I wasn't trying to be insensitive or rude
it's just
you're the **first black guy** I've ever kissed
I don't care what **they** say I think **you're** really fit
my mate would love **you**, **you're** just her type
she doesn't go for guys who are white
she loves **big black guys** so **you'll** do just fine
I promise **you'll** love her
have **you** got any **fit mates or brothers**?
I used to date this **coloured guy**
what a **lovely, lovely guy**
he had these beautiful blue eyes
he was gorgeous and **his d#@k was enormous**
oh my god I miss that **big black c@&K"**
"you what?
why are you telling me this?"
"sorry I wasn't taking the piss!
you just remind me of **him** cus **you** don't act **black**
and neither did **he**—that's what I was getting at
you don't say all that **yo yo** and **brrrap brrrap**
I can't stand all that
you know when **they** chat all that **gangster crap**
I **hate** that—thank God **you're** not like **that**

it's not cus **you're black**
in fact
my mate's **dad's uncle's black**
so is my **dog** and my **cat**
you lot can come back to mine if you **promise you won't nick anything**
I know what you lot are like
I'm watching **you** out the corner of my eye
to be fair I haven't got anything worth
nicking
are **you lot** any good at swimming?
cus I heard **you black guys can't swim**
something about the muscle fibre and the texture of **your skin**"
"yes, I can swim and no I don't want to come in I'm going back see you later lads"
"is it cus I is **white** you don't want to come back?**"**
"no it's cus I'm black
and the fact you can't get past that!!!"

NO HARD FEELINGS

We used to roll together
when
my bankroll was together
when
income was coming in
when
incoming calls kept coming in
when
people kept coming in
until i was running out
then they were running out
funny thing or a money thing
who knows
what a coincidence is?
i didn't even invite them in
yet they still crept in
sipped me like juice and gin
sapped me like a lack of vitamins
used me like Vicodin
it's frightening paranoia heightening

who's real and who's fake
for f#@k sake
i'm not one to swear but i swear i used to swear by them
now
i don't care about them
i've got nothing for or against
we just can't remain mates
no hiding
no hate
friendship dissipates
no more listen mate
no more arguments
not even small talk like parliament
i plead the fifth
but there is no amendment between us
i am no longer your Venus
past experience is just not appealing
like too much consumption
or erectile dysfunction
no hard feelings
and i mean it.

SLEEP LESS

Sleep won't come to me
that's why I'm desperately trying to get to sleep
but sleep is elusive
so hard to get to
so exclusive
tucked away
in the VIP lounge called sleep
I don't even get an invite
never mind a seat
too wired to see
facing the ceiling
with irritable feelings
towards me
now it's 4.40
last time I looked it was 3.43 in the
AM
and I am
so tired
so trying,
trying so hard

but sleep is barred
my mind was fully charged
but now it's slowly losing power
minutes blend into hours
and I've got to be up in two hours
slowly I slip down the slumber tower
and my eyelids start to undulate
like waves
weighed down by their own weight
pupils starting to dilate
if worst comes to worst
my sleep must come first
finally my eyelids meet
longer than a blink, I think?
it feels like sleep
has come to meet and greet
my head starts to hang like a dead arm
yes, sleep is working like a charm
.....beep, beep, beep, beep, beep....
goes my f%$&^&#g alarm.

COMPLEXION COMPLEXITIES
(I CAN SEE)

My complexion comes with complexities
but you know what gets to me?
I wasn't even aware I had a complexion
until negative connections were made about my complexion
made me want a disconnection
from this complexion
and that's when things got complex
way before I lived in a complex
I was commandeered by complexities
and I didn't get them from me
or my family
I was introduced to it by thee
unintelligent emotionally,
and it became me
but I don't blame me
in some ways it made me
at work there were too many maybes
was it them being shady?
because it seems like

my complexion is not up for selection
always in the no promotion section
telling me "I'm an asset, I'm a blessing"
YET when it comes to promotion or pay rise my
chances are somewhat lessened
Don't tell me "I'm playing **that card**"
that card makes me want to punch your face hard
that card I never knew existed
that card that you insist is
exactly what this is
that card that allows you to be dismissive
that card that gives you an excuse not to listen
that card that allows you to turn it around
that card that makes such an annoying sound
when it was you who made the stupid remark
I question you on it
and you say I'm playing the **race card**
how ironic
when it's you who plays on it
case in point
you get mad when Musa and Mo go for salat
so mad you lose your balance
in protest you protest
you think prayer time is an extra break
when **Muslims** are practicing their religion, they pray
five times a day
but cultural ignorance kicks understanding far away

that's why explaining the complexities is so hard
cus you can be **racist** without making a **racist** remark
and of course I can't tell work what I feel from the heart
cus they might sack my claat
victim blaming is one of the great English historical arts
nowadays that history has been passed down to Mark Harriet and John
out of the three there is a blatant **racist** one
a mild and latent one
and a fake caring and patient one
and I must hope one of them takes my complaint seriously
I can see
they're listening
but they're not listening to me
I can see they want to stay clear of me
it would be great if they made space for a **black** or **brown** face
or a person who can relate
when it comes to cultural difference
they understand what **others** have to say
and it gets dealt with it on the day
use it as a teachable moment
make sure conversations are open
this is a multi-cultural nation

you must understand the psychology of representation
to see those that resemble you in position of authority
eradicates the implications of a **minority**
positive image to build self-esteem is priority
knowing that someone understands you
has so much value
what you show us
is what you teach us
beauty and power equals white features
yet you tell me otherwise
yet I don't see any other guys
at the top of the pile
so please forgive my complexities
I say to the white guy next to me
if it makes you uncomfortable talking about "**race**"
step down and make way
it needs **people** who practice anti **racism** in and out of the workplace
as opposed to the whitewashed managers of yesterday
still here today
not much has changed since back in the day
as I look at the **predominantly white managerial wall of silence**
I am muted to **silence**
I must be "professional" and keep my complexities quiet
I just observe the nepotism and hierarchal tyrants

constantly watching the **white English protoype** get promoted
the sure bet always gets the devotion
which evokes unwanted emotion
but I can't let you see me broken
and blatantly bored of the same old, tired uninspired
so, I do like **liars** do and **pretend**
so, I don't offend the **white fragility** brigade
that compose a sympathy symphony serenade
that garners the sycophantic crowd
with their ooohs and arrrs
vociferous and loud
so i am portrayed as the renegade
the perpetrator of the **perpetrator**
hated by the **hater**
bait for the **baiter**
forsaken by the core blatant
and I have no desires
to go round and round like tyres
so I say nothing and stay silent
even though **people of colour** are the global majority
whitewashing labels **black and brown minorities**
to emphasise **whiteness** being autonomous with authority
dishonesty has long replaced integrity and honesty

honestly,
this **white supremacy** pandemic
 devours the workplace
indifference fills the workspace
social standings coerce weak work mates
compliance is the order of the workday
you dare not side with the one being abused
even when you know they've been wrongly accused
for fear of being socially removed
for fear of not being cool with the gang
so, you sit back and take no stance
instead of standing up and doing the right thing
you sit down say nothing and do the "**white thing**"
the fact that you don't even realise this is frightening
and when I point out your inaction
oh dear!!!!
here comes the **white rage** or **white tears**
that's right dear
then I become the target of your hardship
for hearing the truth to your face
then you tell me it has nothing to do with "**my race**"
and you say it with a straight face
and I pretend everything's ok
I just don't want to hear anymore
like Sunshine Anderson i've heard it all before
and yes, you may not have been promoted too
cus the **system** is not designed for me or you

but that's where the comparison stops dude
cus there is one undisputed fact
you've never had the unenviable task
of asking a question where you get the same rhetorical answer back
and that is what complexion complexities will always ask
did this happen to me cus I am **black**?

white privilege means you don't even have to even consider that.

i WRITE

i write when i'm irate
i write when i rate
i write when i **hate**
i write to get the **hate** out
i'm right to get the **hate** out
it's right to get the taste out
my mouth
speaks volumes
that fall on deaf ears
so only a few hear
open-minded **people**
i see only a few here
so, i hope you share
this message loud and clear
if we don't come together
the **hate** will never disappear
they try to segregate us
cus togetherness is what they fear.

TOXIC HOME

Lee and Kerry met in their early 20s
Kerry was pretty, vibrant and slim
to him
that was his taste
they loved immensely
intense lovers and best mates
with age and a baby
she developed shape and waist
for drink,
Lee developed a taste
left Kerry to waste
all cus she went from size eight
to a curvy twelve
Lee started to serve himself
he goes out missing for nights on end
Kerry was left to fend for baby and herself
deteriorated health
she ate more to cope with the stress
she felt a mess
Kerry was a nervous wreck
Lee couldn't care less

partying their allowance away
come home anytime any day
telling her she "looks a state"
calling her "a fat waste of space"
slapping her about the face
anytime he's in a state
of inebriation
intoxicated in a toxic house
Kerry loved Lee but now hates him
she just can't take him
he's nasty and cold like Vinny Jones in his heyday
she wishes his life away
Lee pisses his rights away
to call himself a father
he's now a slave to lager
jaeger bombs earth to Major Tom
on the David Bowie's
he's off his trolley
his attitude sucks like a lolly
with a bitter after taste
he used to be minted like after eights
now Lee's just wank like Master Bates
Kerry's exasperated through anticipated tension
not to mention the 3-year-old who's got a cold and
won't stop crying
and Lee is always on her case
high maintenance

bills to pay
he drank and sniffed the money away
and blames her
for their council state of life
he falls asleep trying to make her cry
Kerry has had enough of this guy
So she takes the knife off the side
mouth open wide
with concentration not to awaken
drunken Lee in a sunken seat
beat down from his daily dose
of 9% cans pipe in his hand
he slumps into a deep imbibed slumber
she wanders over to her 3-year-old
with her clothes
picks her up and gently puts her in her cot
shuts the door no lock
turns the tv up
then sinks the knife into Lee's gut
and twists it in
he exhales with a gasp
mouth aghast
gassed
he asks "why?"
as he tries to grab the knife
while it's slowly taking his life
she cries

and lets the knife go
as his hands release slow
his eyes go
he dies slow
while she cries so hard
saying "you should have loved me for me
so, I'm doing this for me and my baby"
blood-stained hand she picks up her mobile dials 999
confesses and attends to her daughter
she gets 12 years for manslaughter
meanwhile her daughter is farmed out
from house to house
she heard through the rumour mill her Mum killed her Dad
cus he called her "fat"
and she thinks that's that
the daughter thinks that's fact
in fact
it made her bitter and sad
with ill feelings towards her Mum
as she never knew why her Mum had done what she had done
she doesn't know what her Mum had to overcome
she never knew what her Mum had to endure
she never knew her Mum at all
she just thinks her Mum took away her Dad
and what's even more sad

the daughter grows up abused, feeling neglected
now her boyfriend is seriously affected
by her constant need for affection, her need for attention
her need for protection her needs for connection
craving attention feeling insecure
feeling she needed more
always accusing him of cheating
she develops a disorder of eating
she wants to look good for her **man**
she wants to look good for the gram
currently hooked on a gram
a day
her day off is on Saturdays
while he's at work
she's going berserk
when he doesn't answer or reply
straight away
and he's a chilled guy
but he's had this all his adult life
and he's sick of it
so one day he picks up a knife off the side
makes up his mind
to take her life
saying "you made me do it
for years you have been putting me through it
your constant fuming, constantly accusing

constantly hitting me giving me bruises
I was always going to lose it
I can't take your insecurity
why can't you stop calling me
you're not loving me you are stalking me
all the time
I'm going out my mind
anytime I leave mine you call me forty times.
I have no life
I'm stressed from your strife
that's why you could never be my wife"
then picks up the knife that's just took her life
and takes his own
this is the impact of the ripple effect
how one person's actions affect the next
yes
sometimes you're better off leaving to being single and alone
than trying to survive living in a toxic home.

THE PHONE AND ITS FIEND

Long gone is the Kodak moment
sad to say those days are over
the phone has taken over eyes
over time
it's taken over minds
that declined
to live in the moment
the phone is a friend to the fiend
apart,
they are nowhere to be seen
they are as thick as thieves
the phone never leaves
the phone always leads
instructing the fiend to walk and scroll
fiends don't notice traffic or **people** on a stroll
the fiend doesn't notice **people** overall
bumping pedestrians like a ten-pin bowl
the fiend is often totally oblivious
the fiend is often frivolous
the fiend is often found with phone in hand

the fiend is often found with must have brand
the fiend is often air pod wearing
the fiend is often air pod staring
they can't hear a word as their pods are blaring
then they take one ear pod out and snap at you
"*what is it?*"
"I just thought we could talk for a minute"
so, the fiend will talk for an exact minute
then the fiend will put their air pod in meaning conversations finished
then you have the fiend that loves taking pics of d%£*s and sending it to "chicks"
no thought of repercussion in sight
the fiend has no clue that these pics could come back to bite later in life
then we have the filming fiends
all filming the same concert
sat together at concert
it's bonkers
what plonkers
the phone is creating fiends like a machine
I feel slight rage against the fiend
especially the ones who constantly send memes
the phone is taking brains
the fiend takeover is taking place
right in front of my face
exposing intimate moments of privacy

location on, tracking us down, taking liberties
too many fiends' protests for phones out in class
equals
they don't do the English,
they don't learn, they don't pass
so, you do the English and the maths
as it adds
to a whole heap of time wasting
which means a whole heap of minds wasting
on that phone the fiends can't seem to leave alone
but it is the fiend's choice of course
who cares if they fail the course
the phone is more important of course
the phone knows better than the educator or the
source
of course,
i remember the days when we talked
and gathered round
nowadays there's minimal interaction
 and more heads down
essentially
non-entities
dead to the beautiful world
dead to the beautiful pearl
with a wonderful waft
that just walked past
beautiful moments so often passed

lost in the glass of the phone screen
 in a fiend phone dream
fixated in a trancelike state
so, i rest my case
that covers my phone
i let it sit there all alone
 away from my dome
cus i don't want to be cloned
caught in the current
 floating down the mainstream
all aboard with the phone fiends
existing as an addict
with arms like go go gadget
every time the phone rings
I won't grab it when it's near
hence why it's on silent
i remember the days when phones were only for the ear
now the phone has got an i in
Steve was on his Job
so, fiends buy in
admiring
like it's the Apple of their eye
tapping apps and text styling
semi writing words, auto correct typing
who needs a brain for spelling and writing?
the phone has taken the fiends right in
that's why i had to document this in writing

much like a reporter
I see fiends take their phones in the steam room and sauna
when it's a time for switching off
they're always turned on
the phone is their turn on
if the fiend turns left, i go right
take in life and vibe
take my time,
ease my mind
as these thoughts tease my mind
seeing fiends having tantrums when their battery dies
pleading strangers for a charger as if for dear life
if there is no phone reception
the fiend often has no connection
with human life
until of course, the fiend sees the light.

HERSELF

She walks with an air of grace
with no heirs and graces
she is gracious
from head to feet
gracious in defeat
her beauty is understated
she is open to topics outside of her bubble
her intelligence is blatant
when she speaks your attention is taken
she doesn't crave likes
she craves life
she is secure in herself
others doubt themselves around her
females find her hard to work out
jealousy all around her
she has emotional intelligence
and a great figure
she exercises her mind, go figure
she often has her hair draped up
lip gloss no makeup
defining features

that most hide with blusher foundation
and bleaches
she teaches the underprivileged
which became her dream job
following her peers down the corporate route
isn't what she dreamed of
as she grew her lifelong friends became few
they drifted apart as she found paths a new
she is content being alone
when others needed to be in a crew
she never wants to
she doesn't need them to satisfy her soul
she is satisfied and whole
her presence can satisfy you whole
she is dependent on her independence
she doesn't want a partner to define her
or divide her
she is her own provider, a true rider
she represents herself, humanity and gender
she never has an agenda
far from a great pretender
she is one
at one with herself
rarely asks for help
but always there to help
she does what she feels like doing
she is being herself.

IN LAW

The law means nothing
for many in law
they start with love for the law
then work their way up the law
to the lofty height
of thinking they are above the law
but for those who don't do as bad as those in law
they are called outlaws
yet those who work in law
play outside laws
while we are not free outside doors
cameras everywhere we turn
in the house of law
authorities are supposedly the most honest and lawful
for many innocents they are lawless and awful
when the accused works for the state
they proceed with caution
corroborating, cover ups, lies and extortion
impious and biased
with no conscience
tons of evidence omitted

the law is nonsense
the guilty official is often acquitted
in exchange for
innocent lives being fitted
for crimes not committed
the court of <u>law</u> excels in token gestures
"do you solemnly swear under oath"
what a joke
from a load of jesters
purely for show
and that show must go on
they swear on principles
out of principal that they don't adhere to
many are not even near to
the place or **people** they claim to be
the place that's devoid of humanity
the institutional **wall of silence** stretches to great lengths
to hide its vanity
in the house of justice
just .....is
justice
if it's just them
but definitely
not just
if it's just us
it just is

rarely ever justice
that's why it must be
just we
cus we can't rely on eyes of guys
that just see
what they've been programmed to see
what they've been probing to see
what they've been hoping to see
even with body cams, these poor enforcers
don't hide the evil forces
they are institutionalised
with institution eyes
innocent **people** coerced
into admitting crimes, they didn't commit
and having to do time
it's sick
the **good old boys**' club have everyone in line
woe betides
if anyone steps outside
the whistleblower gets attacked
so the establishment stays intact
and the good work for the bad
moral and ethics lack
especially when black/brown and white working class
the law will hold you back
until it's a matter of **white male** "upper" class
notice how they care for those they **class**

as their own
they never break the **class code**
they use **colour sexuality and gender** to distract loads
but it's time **people** should realise
we are all on the same side
especially when millions of innocent lives
are wrongly incarcerated
by a **system** perniciously inaugurated
historically rooted in **greed classism**, obligatory
bigotry, **nepotism** and **prejudice**
opposed to what the institution is supposed to be
opposed to what they said it is
when the **system** is **incredulous**
corrupt officials brag boastfully
for literally getting away with murder
on the back of that
this should really disturb you
they get a pat on the back
in front of cameras and the **media** pack
praised for being "brave"
for **shooting** a **man** in the back who was running away
or a **gang of cops pinning** a person to the floor
and **beating** him till he can't move anymore
instead of deescalating the situation
they create more
that's what they call fulfilling duties
these idiots really think we are blind and stupid

we can see their sick ways
and to add insult to injury
they get suspended with pay
even some promotions are made
the institution increases their pay
or they get transferred to another place
just so that the institution can save face
which is an absolute disgrace
law enforcers always want civilians to snitch
calling them informants
treated with importance
but if a colleague snitches on another colleague
they are called a bitch
and ostracised by the hypocrites
so, the bad apples that rot the core
rarely ever get thrown away
they bruise the **system** and spread decay
and there continues the **corruption** that goes on
and affects every institution to this day
corruption is rife especially in the UK and USA
which is detrimental to we the **people** in every way.

'Injustice anywhere is a threat to justice everywhere' MLK

CLASS

i'm in a **class** of my own
i don't want to be in the **class** of clones
who can't stand to sit alone
who love to lower the tone
as they gather round
and get loud
taking turns to be **class** clown
if one gets their back up
they know they've got back up
so, they can't be seen to "back down"
in their local their so brave
fuelled by drink and **class** A's
they **stare** and **gaze**
which is why I coined the phrase
the smaller the town
the bigger the frown
with an unclassified **class mentality passed down**
so, with a bit of **class**
i go up
to bring them back down.

INGER-LAND

It goes from glory to gory
united we celebrate
make a mistake, lose
then comes a hell of **hate**
the **Inger-lish** don't stick together
like Sellotape
It goes from "it's coming home"
to "no you fucking won't"
to violent moans and groans
smashed cups
drunk, buzzed, zoned
with the *In ger land* predictable **racist** tone
these basic barbaric brains
these basic barbaric clones
vacant heads easily entertained
drained of individualism
three *African* lions on **Inger-land** twerps
tones of imperialism hurt
those they once cheered
go from "here, here!!"
to a few beers

to a few smokes
to a few pokes of coke
and then that bloke
becomes that bloke
that jokes about
choking, groping, beatings, cheating
berating the opposition
hating the opposition
with their **xenophobic** version of **nationalism**
bellowing at the television
with every sip
with every sniff
their volume goes up a bit
one of them proper pissed
as he kissed his first can
at 6.46
in the AM
now he's swaying
it's still four hours till kick off
chanting, arm raised clapping
showing his bits off
before the kick off
predictable as **Brits abroad** in flip flops
yes, this lot
of the **so called first world**
are truly from the **worst world**
that call themselves **supporters**

raising **sons** and **daughters**
even winning can turn into a fight
when losing the good vibe goes goodbye
and those so-called good guys
turns into **thug** guys
looking for **people** to fight
smashing up their local
vocal and woeful
yet **proud**
sing the **national anthem**
then **boo** the opposition loud
brave cowards in groups
truth and common sense aloof
place full of **anger**
the absence of joy in view
abundance of bravery through **booze**
"It's **their** fault we lost the fucking final
I'm **getting one** of **them fuckers**
and that's fucking final
if it wasn't for **them**
we would have won the fucking European title
it's vital we get **one** at least
let's just fuck **one** up for no reason
yes, **he's fucking bleeding**"
steaming in with punches and kicks
<u>to get their kicks</u>

<u>to get their fix</u>
beating a defenceless guy senseless
cus common sense is senseless
amongst the senseless
black and brown people collectively wince when
a **black player misses**
Inger land historical echoes
of **rhetorical racist disses** and **hisses**
are as inevitable
as *In ger land* going home to **beat up his Mrs**
whom he never misses
the **sexist, homophobic, racist, bigot**
who's got **"black and brown mates"** but calls them
p#£"s and **n!$%*&s**
behind their back
the ones that always say *"you know i'm not like that"*
Yes**, those two-faced t%"&s**
that are enabled to blend into society
where **skin colour** is never associated with **his variety**
that **call themselves men**
but don't deserve the title
we must call out any form of **bigotry**
when we see or hear it ...it's vital
they say it's a "**small minority**"
which is clearly **ignored** by the **"majority"**
as it's still not been eradicated

by we the **people** or the **"authorities"**
racism has been around for **centuries**
so, it seems more like a **white propensity**
to not do as they say
talk about doing sweet **F.A**
that's not fair play
as this **disease** has been **enabled**
by **institutions** disabled
and **devoid** of doing things for a good cause
unless there is something in it for them of course
we need to kick it out ourselves
we can't wait for thsoe that are there for self
they don't walk the walk all they do is talk
thats why we need to stand up
woman and **man** up
lifting
it's the only way to kill this thing
we all must invest time
to align our morals equally
this is much bigger than the game
we can't rely on their token gesture campaigns
we together can kick out this culture of **hate**
and we can evolve easily and peacefully
when WE all stand up for, WE
that's the ENGLAND I long to see

BRICKS AND MORTAR

They say blood is thicker than water
but not when it comes to bricks and mortar
no time for son, mother and daughter to breathe
let alone grieve
thieves in plain sight
using the family name for selfish gain
their only plight
is to conquer and divide
get their share
without care
it would seem
for the loss of a supposed loved one
where has all that love gone?
where has all that blood gone?
they say blood is thicker than water
but not when it comes to bricks and mortar
no time for son, mother and daughter to breathe
let alone grieve
one dies
one family become two tribes
one side wants to look after the family properly

while the other side wants hands on the family property
looking for the golden ticket to the lottery
not a tear in sight
just fights
who's having the cars
who's having the bike
parents and siblings of the deceased
all they want is their piece
while the wife and children want their peace
the line has been drawn in the sand
now everyone knows where they stand
parents and siblings want the upper hand
trying to leave the wife and children in no man's land
but that's not the plan
so, they leave it in the karma god's hands
they say blood is thicker than water
but not when it comes to bricks and mortar.

WHITE WALL OF SILENCE

I hear your **silence** from a mile off
you witness **injustice** and you **sly off**
pretending you don't know it exists
your **silence** is the reason it persists
pretending you can't see or hear it
like **compliance** is your gift
when I see **people** like you my mood shifts
I see you're not moved
it's
clear you don't give a shit
and that's what hurts
you're just not stirred
as long as you are ok
as long as you get paid
there is no way you are going to **speak up**
and that's why I don't want to know or meet up
with the likes of you
the irony is if it was the other way around
I would fight for you.

KNIFE DOWN

"Put the knife down son
you don't need it
put the knife down son
you're bleeding"………….
(two months earlier)
there lived a guy called Mez
never in any major trouble not known by the Feds
he was popular in the ends always on his ped
he got and gave respect
he was a good kid
lived with his big sis
younger brother, mother and part time father
hence why his Mum was out a lot
working hard to provide
so they had a decent life
the most Mez did was drink
with the guys
in the park till it got dark
smoked his vape
blaze the haze
watching his mates get loud and messy

egged on and fuelled by Jess aka Jessy
who was the older and much colder
he'd done time nuff times
but he never stopped shotting for a living
had some youngsters riding with him
or should i say for him
he was Icey dripped so they adored him
he got the Jordans for Jordan
and the Cavalli's for Kimani
anytime they went out he'd buy all the rounds
acted like he owned the town
he would line up the lines
saying "the world is mine"
quoting a Scarface line
show them a good time
give them stuff on tick
then after party back at his
he'd give them a tour like MTV Cribs
Jessy would tell them to invite their mates round
then he'd talk their mates round
then they'd do the rounds
for those sterling pounds
which he would take his main cut
but if his cut was cut short
he'd take a cut out of them
saying "I'm not your friend
I'm not your boy I'm your boss

I draw the line at a loss
that's a line you better not cross"
Jessy always carried knives
bragged about taking lives
he made slit throat gestures
"this ain't no joke and I ain't no jester"
he'd shout as a threat
high
he loved to get
cocaine was his choice of drug
the more he had the more he'd thug
he had a psychological hold on the youngers
his line was "family is amongst us"
making them feel the part
making them feel a part of something
manipulating them from the start
he was evil and smart
meanwhile Mez had got himself in a mess
with a tough guy who tried to test
rule no 1 you can't show fear in the ends
so, Mez got heated
in the end
the situation went from calm to not cool
the guy Mez had beef with always carried tools
and he doesn't want to get caught slipping on the way
to school
he tells a mate who tells him to call Jessy

so, he does, and Jessy says he will sort it before it gets messy
on the condition Mez returned Jessy's deed
unlike Santan Dave
Mez wanted to dead that beef
Mez reluctantly agrees
a few weeks later Mez gets a call
from an unknown caller
Mez walks down the hall
Away from his family
sat in the front room happily unaware
Jess is calling Mez for a favour no doubt
as Jess has sorted the beef out
he said "it's light work you'll be in and out"
so, Mez gives Jess his address
Jessy texts "i will be there late afternoon bless"
Mez gets a next text from Jess
saying "make sure you wear black
I will holla you when I'm round the back"
Two hours pass Jessy texts saying "come out"
Mez shouts to the house
he's just nipping out
before he got a shout back
Mez is out the door quicker than Kyle Walker at right back
Jessy is sat back in a black hatchback
black hoody black Skully

with black hat to the back
mouth covered with black bandana over that
you could only see his eyes
he flashes his lights twice
late afternoon turned into early night
Mez gets in his whip
he can see that Jessy's lit
car filled with smoke
he pulls out some coke from his coat
he puts it in a zoot, tells Mez to take a toke or two
Mez has a few hits
and after a few
Mez feels lit
Jessy takes some big hits
like a boxer losing on points
then he points
"you see that down there
handle it with care
It's my gift to you
now here's what I want you to do"
after a thirty-minute drive
they arrive outside a block of council flats
Jessy says "take that pack
under the chair
go deliver it right there
where the light is
next to where that bike is

don't be frightened
I'm right here"
without fear Mez says "pass it here"
takes the pack and walks away
he looks back at Jessy
who mouths "go bro you're blessed"
Jessy waves him away with the back of his hand
mouthing "you da **man**"
as Mez gets closer the light goes off
a guy dressed all in black comes out
and sounds off
Mez is shook no doubt
but doesn't show any fear
cus he knows Jessy's near
but when he looks back Jessy's disappeared
Mez gets to the guy and the guy says drop it
so he drops it and quickly walks away
but his path is blocked right away
Mez is at a complete loss
he can't believe Jessy has driven off
now surrounded by guys in black ballies
one guy runs at Mez madly
so, Mez lunges at him badly
now the guy is lagging
his mates are so scared they don't back him
they all dip and start running
the guy falls holding his stomach

2 Outspoken

Mez is statuesque and flummoxed
looking at the guy losing his life
Mez has stabbed him with a knife in the stomach and chest
the knife was the present from Jessy
blood is pouring from the lad,
he's bleeding bad
laying their lifeless
nobody expected it to end like this
the knife is locked in Mez's hand
this was not what he planned
he looks at the guy
he looks at the knife
he can't believe this is his life
flashing before him
with the victim fading away
he can hear sirens are blazing away
the blue disco lights are in sight
Mez's adrenaline has come and gone
the buzz is wearing off
then Mez feels a sharp pain
he looks down in vain
his black hoody is bloody
Mez didn't realise he too had been stabbed
and his wound is pretty bad
from the back
he hears "put the knife down son

you don't need it
put the knife down son
you're bleeding"
Mez falls to the ground
let's out an almighty sound
like a wounded hound
as the police surround
he goes down
an officer gives him mouth to mouth
Mez takes one big gasp
but alas it's his last.

GET OUT

i had to get out from this social media obsession
to avoid social media depression
bored of too many **people** professing possessions
shiny things make big impressions
like two big melons
shooting for the stars like a Smith and Wesson
absorbed by looks
abhor books
I just see
people so lusty
for obligatory likes
for the likes of fabricated looks
muscles, bust and butts
but
what is it all for?
virtual reality on all fours
getting shafted by attention whores
much more than a metaphor
but who am I to judge
to each their own
but that's my point

there are too many clones
not enough minds work alone
and they don't get the scent
even if you wore cologne
they struggle to be individuals
they'll never walk alone
can't see many originals
hence why I had to get out
with my angst
I had to let out
and give thanks
I gave my mind a chance
say it as I see
as opposed to what they want me to see
monopolised media outlets are infecting
an alternative perspective
that's often disrespected
by those that have perfected
cognitive dissonance
not interested in listening
that's why it's good to step away from the herd
so that you can hear yourself be heard
you can hear more than one word
and stop one version immersing
the more diversity you seek to socialise with
the more you are understanding and learning
the more you/we are earning

the more sources you research the more informed
the less you research the more you are formed
when you believe the first thing you're told
the same lies never get old
just rebranded and resold
and you get took by the crooks
I see good looks, great frames
with bland brains obsessed with brand names
looking for a stake to claim
looking for great acclaim
I see looks
that looks the same
I see pics
frame by frame
influenced by an influencer with no influence
It's contagious like influenza
aww bless ya
but it's nothing to sneeze at
i'm pleased that
you're having fun
you're making a ton
you feel like you belong
and you're getting the attention
i'm just getting at the intention
and if you have never thought about that
I thought it worth a mention
as i feel like i'm banging my head against a sick wall

and i'm a patient on a sick ward
i'm not supposed to be on
i try to shed light as bright as neon
but they scroll past
to lovely Leonie and Leon
who get the obligatory "oh love it"
"oh i like it"
"The perfect couple, omg I'm so excited"
can't wait to see you hotties at Wireless"
the lust for looks is tireless
overindulged in aesthetics
must be pleasingly athletic
and I realise oh my oh my
words can't compete with the eye
especially when the eye
doesn't have to try
as it's wined and dined
in a filter of shallow lies
that mesmerise
and the truth is just an eyesore
that's pushed out of sight
but i
did try
the most to refocus
but it was hopeless
talking to a plague of low-cost minds
with trimmed stomachs and high-class behinds

2 Outspoken

I try to open minds
but it's like talking to the blinds
with nobody behind
its curtains
certain waste of time
so, I take mine
and my mind
to where I can learn
where the lines aren't blurred
I managed to get out
So, i'm here to spread the word

WATERFALL

i fight that water that tries to flood my eyes
but my eyes are drowning so my efforts are futile
so many years of water being held up by my masculinity dam
experience and empathy made my dam burst
now i don't give a damn
if the water falls like a waterfall
to my surprise
a wave of relief sits beneath
my tear infused cheeks
see
as a **man** of my era
i put my hand up like Alan Shearer
to celebrate my gradual alleviation of **toxicity**
that spreads across cities like **atrocities**
messages are misconstrued
views miscued
blurred vision skewed
words misused
the scapegoats abused
insults feel like a permanent bruise

but i never let the water fall
i couldn't let them see a tear drop
i couldn't let them see what my fear was
instead of them helping **man** up
they'd say, "**man** down" and tell you to "**man** up"
thankfully that's all in the past now
i won't let that mentality **pass down**
looking back, i must admit
the way those words hit
made my tears quit
until i understood the matrix
i took the red pill
like Morpheus
i overstand the societal ills
I realise there's much more for us
now i let my water spill
if needs be
if my tears need me
i will let them fall freely
for me to be me
i need to be free of **toxic** traits
that get served on **toxic** plates
day to day
that are not to my taste
at one point i digested it
feelings left festering
for fear of ridicule by silly fools

following silly rules
over the years i let peers go
over time i let those years go
so
if i feel the water coming
i let my water fall and my tears flow.

JUST DESERTS

They say blood is thicker than water
well, wait till an **abuser** marries your parent, brother, sister, son or daughter
the **devil** dilutes that blood into pink water
as the **abuser** is so far into the **abused** head
the **abused** brain is laden with dread
with loyalty as thick as lead
so when it comes to the **abused** vulnerability
when the **abused** shows it
the **abuser** knows it
then the **abuser** will expose it
doing everything to **look good** in front of the in-laws
indoors the **abuser** is an **outlaw**
the **abuser** is on best behaviour outdoors
like the **abuser's** public persona is outsourced
the **abuser** is an **emotional user**
sucking out the **abused** soul like a hoover
psychologically moulding the **abused** like clay
turning the **abused** into their **slave**
saying they need to **be trained**
attached to a **psychological chain**

unbiased eyes point this out to the loved one
telling the **abused** this is an **abuser not a good one**
but this often backfires
external intervention is not what the **abused** or the **abuser** desires
but little does the **abused** know it's what's required
for the **abused** sake family take a step back
for the **abused** sake there is no step back
from the **sociopathic narcissist**
the **abused** can only hope that karma plays a huge part in this
as the **abuser** likes to isolate their **prey**
friends of the **abused** don't get to see them from day to day
visitors look the other way
while the **abuser taunts its prey**
all family can do is pray
abusers never change
but **they** expect the **abused** to **remain the same**
and change depending on the day
the **abuser** must always **have their way**
or the **abused** will always pay
it must be hard to admit the **abused** has made a mistake
when **love is at stake**
external opinion swept away
the **abused** own thoughts are **kept at bay**
as the **abused** doesn't want to upset the **demon**

when the **abuser** is a male "parent", they are just a donor of semen
when the **abuser** is a female "parent" they are just carriers of children
traumatising offspring for life
insecure **abusers control** lives
that don't concern **them**
controlling body, clothes, mind, soul, outings and earnings
the **abused** is yearning for the **abuser**'s love
the **abuser** knows this and is burning the book
the **abuser** is nothing but a **crook**
who knows nothing about love
the abuser uses any **tactic** they can to make the **abused compliant**
from **physical violence**
to a **psychological tyrant**
using **manipulative** words and or **complete silence**
whatever **trick** the **abuser** uses there is a complete science
the abuser's disguise is exposed in their **abusive** eyes
abusers are truly **evil guys**
both genders apply
and the **abused** often can't see past
the **abused** is busy looking for good
the **abused** can't see bad
too busy trying to get love back
from a low-level **hood rat**

who needs trapping
the **abuser** needs catching
and when they do
there'll be no one to back **them**
because this **type** has no true friends
the only hope is the **abused** gets a happy end
or the **abuser** get their **just deserts** in the end.

NOT THE RIGHT TIME

Sorry now's just **not the right time**
im concerned for your welfare not just mine
we take everything you say seriously
i'm sure they didn't mean it seriously
you need to **manage your expectations**
i just....haven't got time for an explanation
yes, but what was the actual **allegation**?
i'm afraid this will be **too time consuming**
oh no i think they were trying to be amusing
i think that's where there's been some confusion
i'm sorry now's just **not the right time**
if you're that bothered make an **official complaint**
online
make sure you channel your **aggression**
i mean **your expression** in the right way
try **toning** it down I'd say
fine do it **your way**
i just don't want you to regret anything you might say
you know **we value your hard work and commitment** to the cause
but i'm afraid that's up to a **court of law**

2 Outspoken

I've never heard them say anything like that before
you've caught me at the **wrong time**
we will have to catch up some time
see you later ok
make sure you **say it in the right way**
you are deemed quite **aggressive** i'd say
and this meeting is not about **racism or prejudice**
i'm not trying to be **incredulous**
this isn't me trying to **shut you down**
if you want it on the agenda you have to write it down
we may not even get time to finish at this rate
this is a **piss take**
how come **they get special treatment**
your hair is a bit.... well it
doesn't look.....**aesthetically pleasing**
there is a **place** and a **time** to talk about **these things**
I want you to know **we do care about these things**
but now's just **not the right time**
systemic oppression?
yea right!!
i don't need a lecture or a lesson alright
just **be grateful** you've got a job
 that's a blessing
i'm sure they didn't mean to be offensive they were only messing

unfortunately, I've not got time to meet him
so feel free to **arrange your own meeting**
in your own time
preferably around home time
i'm sure she's sorry for her actions
if we concentrate on that it'll be a distraction
if you don't react, all will be fine
i'd love to help you but **now's** just **not the right time**.

DISS CUSSERS

I dislike the **diss cussers**
cus you **diss cuss people** when they are not
in the discussion
if they're not there to defend themselves
then it's **disgusting**
that you **diss cuss** them
especially when you've never told them
yet you scold them
behind their back
never mind the fact
they're none the wiser
so they don't get the point
like Pfizer
I'd advise ya to get an advisor
a lot wiser
than you
they will tell you to your face
to "tell them to their face"
be wary of what the **diss cusser diss cusses** with whom
be wary of the **diss cussers** room

in the house of the **diss cussers** crew
or you could be in disgusting **diss cussers** stew
as **diss cussers** will be **diss cussers** you
the same way too.

Diss cussers *are individuals who avoid direct confrontation, choosing instead to diss and cuss others behind their backs through gossip, lies and hyperbole. Their aim isn't to resolve conflicts or educate but to seek attention, cause havoc, and turn people against someone they may feel intimidated by or simply don't like, even if no wrong was done to them.*

THE PEOPLE: PART I

To get the **people**
the government must get to the **sheeple**
to look like they are there for the **people**
but the sheeple work against the **people**
which equals we the **people**
dividing us into factions of the **people**
which makes fractions of the **people**
which equals we the **people**
fighting against the **people**
taking power from the **people**
instead of condemning the **people**
that **instigate** and **perpetuate** the **evil**

THE PEOPLE: PART II

They pay the **sheeple** to invade the **people**
to play the **people** off
the **sheeple** do the dirty work
for their dirty boss
who couldn't give a dirty toss
about the **people**
at a dirty loss
the **sheeple** pass off
as "just doing their job"
but that's just
not just
it's just not
it's just a cliché
it's just a line
because morals and ethics are not aligned
when you are on the wrong side
aiding greedy guys
to sustain these divides
I don't know why
the **sheeple** can't use their eyes
I feel like kicking off like a guest on Jeremy Kyle

2 Outspoken

I'm riled
seeing so much apathy and denial
in TV the **sheeple** invest
letting brain cells rest
when they say
 "it's for the best
it's in the **people**'s interest"
the **sheeple** just accept
so, the **sheeple** ingest
then the **sheeple** invest
in whatever's being said
no matter if it's at the expense of the **people**
the **sheeple** regress
the **sheeple** always say "yes"
so, they can always make out we are in a mess
and they are going to save us from the mess
may I suggest?
the **people** who govern us are not our friends
but they create fear then pretend to amend
they make enemies of those they befriend
yet the **sheeple** never seem to notice
could it be because their lens is smudged or unfocused
could it be the **sheeple** couldn't care less
as long it's not them being dressed down
the **people** are happy to be addressed
by a robot "appropriately" dressed
telling you the worst

like they want the best
if the media were wearing a dress
it would seem the **sheeple** always think its seamless
and it seems less
are noticing the threads
that always lead to that same killer dress
so easily the **sheeple** believe
so easily impressed
looking at the story because it got legs
from a perverted view
the **sheeple** don't notice the informer also wears
and always has the same views
different anchor on every channel
yet it's the exact same news
the **sheeple** agree and share the same view
without a clue
they win again
and the **people** lose
I despise these parasites that suck lives
with clickbait for their online paper to sell
hope their front page is waiting in hell
I'm raging as well. Misery loves company
and misery loves to make money for companies
hence why wisely, I choose my company
so, misery doesn't come for me
I believe in karma so that comforts me
I believe there are more good **people** than bad

that's comforting
but more of us need to confront this thing
called **corruption**
we need a major interruption
from we the **people**
to eradicate this evil
the cost of living always goes up
yet our wage barely does
then they blame the 0.5 percent
and tell the **sheeple** that's where all the money went
then **sheeple** go outside hotels to vent
how can the **sheeple** be so dense?
it's easy to believe when it's not you being suspected
it's easy to hate when you feel disconnected
brainwashed by false images projected
we need to be aware and stay connected
if you really want to follow the pounds
you've got to punch up not down
get mad at the 1% that f us around
and stay level as one on the ground
together as the **people**
with all due respect there is no sequel
if we all come together now
it's power to the **people**.

SHH THE FOOTY'S ON

All i want to do is watch the football
i don't want to be disturbed by f all
not even to answer a phone call
i thought you were going to have a bath now
i even put out your favourite bath towel
i laid the mats out
so why do you want to chat now?
shhh the footy's on that's that now
i just want to watch the game in peace
now you want to show your flaming fleece
not now please
i told you the game starts at three
and now of all times you want to trouble me
can't you show me when the adverts are on?
oooops.... sorry you can't it's on BBC one
Gary Lineker, Ian Wright, Micah Richards and Roy
oh boy
"why does that Roy slag players off?"
"that's his job"
and it's one hell of a panel
hell, no i'm not changing the channel

i want to hear their analytical opinion
i don't care what your goody bags have got in them
please move out the way i want to see the rest of the line up
so now you decide to put the blinds up
are you on a wind up?
why do you care that i want to see the formation?
please, not now, i'm starting to lose patience
why are you ringing your mate in here?
chat in the kitchen please and grab us a beer
okay don't bother then
go next door and bother them
or just chill here in silence
i will return the favour if you are quiet
right, they've kicked off
cus of you i've missed all the pre match
damn i'm pissed off
ninety plus minutes of peace
is all i ask?
so please, stick to the task.

CASH POINT

Your point of cash is the cash point
but how much does the cash point you
like a camera getting flash
is that the point of cash?
so, one can point at cash
making a point of cash
to be Ludacris jumping in pools to make a big splash
is it to build up a big stash to stash
for a rainy day
what will cash make you do?
what will cash make you say?
i've seen cash point **people**'s morals look the wrong way
just to get paid
or a rise in wage
i've seen cash make **people** stay
when they should have gone that day
and they're still there till this day
cash points wrongns the wrong way
i've seen cash turn **people** into slaves
in this day and age

they will do anything they are told
i've seen warm **people** turn cold
i've seen **people** wave, look amazed
as they do the cash point
at the guy with the flash joint
and a flash car
the cash pointers treat him like a cash star
when it comes to cash i'd rather rock the casbah
then get into a clash over cash
it's funny what cash does to **people**
they say cash is the root of all evil
i say it's only when it's in the hands of evil **people**
that always make c.r.e.a.m
so, cash rules everything around me
i call it a nightmare. The United States calls it a dream
only for certain **people** it would seem
for those that feel insecure
they feel cash is the cure
but they're addicts so they always want more
when is enough, enough?
why do some need ridiculous amounts of cash to "live good"?
while others live rough
all cus the cash point had too much for them
while for others it never had enough
insufficient funds
insufficient love

many live and die in the buff
too many diamonds in the Sierra Leone rough
being took for cash by hungry European crooks
making children do their dirty work
about them they couldn't a f@#k
no mention of slave labour
as long as the cash point is making paper
the cash pointers get their crooked accountant to fiddle
the dirty books
some of the biggest cash points are the biggest corpo-
rate c u next Tuesday
It's rude they
poison the food that we munch
these crooks
lessen the quantity
and they up the price
for "food" that doesn't suffice,
read all labels is my advice
before you buy
before you die
they give us crap en masse
that don't nourish or sustain
the crap that goes into mass productions
is insane
they sign lives away like treaties
overpriced sugar saturated food
in exchange for diabetes

sugarcane is sure gain
notice how they cancer research
over and over again
with decades of research
how come they still haven't found a "cure"
that cancer research must be really poor
and lab "researchers" are part of the cash point game
people are still getting cancer
corporate companies are to blame
the pharma companies are calmer companies
when they've got sick **people** to play
and they've got sick **people** to pay
who sell their palliative medicines that keep the doctor away
for a few days
the cash point is their life it's their way
to add insult to illness they are rarely made to pay
and the greed is getting worse each day
so, if you don't pay attention
it will cost thee
we can't afford to not see
cus if you ignore the games, they play
the cash point will be very costly.

DIFFERENT

You're scared to have a **different opinion**
but what's the point in copying opinions
if there's no truth in them?
why would I want to be like you?
when I can be like me
see,
they give us labels
that enable
or unable us
you're told **"you're not able" for being labelled disabled**
when they don't know if you are able
to be identified we should define our own identity
as we are individual entities
with **different** experience, **different** sensory
only I can censor me
freedom has been sold to us for centuries
and the masses have bought into it
oh, the irony
we are all **immigrants** who arrived at **different** times
so, we are all on **different** times

now it's a **different** time
I don't control yours and you don't control mine
which is why I always like to take my time
cus it's my time to take
I just hope the next generation has a **different** way of thinking
where **different nationalities**, religion, ethnicity and **skin colour** don't distort their way of thinking
we all have **different** ways
different experiences make **people** behave **different** on **different** days
give me a choice of living with generic or **different**
different stays
embracing **different** ways
we can do this in many **different** ways
knowing **difference** gives you something **different** to say
something **different** to play
something **different** to do
different gives **people** a **different** truth
different cultures, **different** tastes
love and **hate** should not be determined by a **different colour** body and face
different hips, **different** tones, **different** shapes
difference is there to embrace
when you dismiss a **different** point of view
difference points at you
cus we can all be cohesive and **different** too.

JOBSWORTH

Watch out for the jobsworth
making more effort than the job's worth
feel like giving them a gob's worth
but they turn on the sob works
when confronted
yet they watch you like the hunted
waiting for you to slip up
that's when they nip up
stairs
telling anyone
who cares
about a *"minor misdemeanour"*
I can't stand their demeanour
as they look you in the eye
say "you're a good guy"
getting bosses to say "goodbye"
behind your back
get you sacked
get you backed
into a corner
they don't have the decency to warn ya

thus
they throw you under the bus
then get on it and ride home
leaving you high, dry and lone
squashed and deflated
while they're in the staff room elated
chatting sweet nothings to the next plaintiff
alliance they're gaining
unbeknown they'll be complaining
about them next
that's why I'm vexed
cus there's no need
for your dud deeds
trying to gain favour from your superiors
instead of designing your own interior
you want to feel big and make others feel inferior
only cus I'm a word's worth
I put it into words worth
but you're less than my word's worth
but I had to write more than a word's verse
trying not to curse
on how adverse
a penny's worth
in a penny purse
you sit
trying to make change
in a bad way

trying to make it a bad day
if you do a good job
great
but stop trying to make others bait
if you really have their best interests at heart
why not be honest from start?
talk to the person in question
come with some helpful suggestions
and if they don't adhere
then my dear
warn them
but don't storm them
without any warning
so they're gone by the morning
let them know where they stand
instead
you want to be a one **man** band
it's dead
blowing your own trumpet
for your own comfort
trying to boost your self-esteem
how about help the team
and stop trying to stitch **people** up
stop trying to switch **people** up
and do us all a favour
check your behaviour
at the door

before
you enter the building
cus tempers are building
towards you
so before they turn on you
think how much your job's worth
and stop being a f'&*^$!g jobsworth.

NAH MAN

Our vernacular is very biased towards "**Man**"
like a male word shower
like we need more "**manpower**"
here's a bit of a list
that sounds like **women don't exist**
when i wear a satchel it's a "**Man bag**"
damn that
Man, you're not "**Man enough**"
Man, "i thought i was"
now you've got to **prove it**
like grabbing something heavy and **move it**
if one has a **skinny physique**
some consider it "**unmanly**" and "**weak**"
which is why some go to the gym weekly
so they're not seen as "**weakly**"
"**real Men** don't **cry**"
why?
is the **show of emotion** connected to **gender**?
so many **Men** play the **great pretender**
some **Men** are fobbed off
for not having a "**real Man's job**"

or ridiculed for having a "**small Man's**"
knobheads
putting **manhoods** to the test
they reply, "**Man's good**"
when **Man's dead** inside his head
peer pressure you regret
want to forget
i mean what's **Man's** obsession with **Man**
"**Man up Man down
Man of the match**"
this is a "**Man's world**"
and if you don't "**Man up**"
you're a "**damn girl**"
like being the **opposite sex** is an insult
cliche overindulge
so, **Man** hasn't always got to try it
so, **Men** we need to try this
and leave **Man** out of it
and **allow the bias**.

THESE PEOPLE HATE

Hate comes in many different forms
hate forms where **hate** is spawned
parents poisoning their roots
infecting their youth
placing their children in future danger
telling them to treat "**others**" like strangers
the strangest advice you could give to a child
wild, that they think they are being **good people**
by injecting evil into their seed
with **hate** speech they **hate** teach
it makes me so sad that girl or that lad
only relates to certain mates
of a certain **white** "**race**"
that look or sound a certain way
growing up to **hate black** and **brown** faces
from the UK and colonised **black** and **brown** places
parroting their parents' **hatred**
to **black** and **brown** faces
and the **black** and **brown** faces haven't been raised
with hatred
the **black** and **brown** faces haven't been raised as

racists
and they find it hard to take it
so the **white face** gets confronted
and the **black** and **brown** face gets insulted
by being called the **aggressor**
by the **prejudiced** head **suppressor**
and the **white face** who made the **abhorrent comment**
is off the hook like an inedible fish
they do as they wish
thrown back into the **white sea**
swim away from captivity
the issue gets typically **brushed under the carpet**
no constructive conversations started
just another wasted teachable moment
they'd rather not face it
especially when the issue is **racist**
it's a case of
that case goes to the bottom
of the bottom draw
sat on top of many more
and they think they are **good people**
their motto says "**treat everyone equal**"
they do when it comes to certain **people**
so the parents of the **racially assaulted** don't believe you
without action that motto is see through
so, the school gets reported, and it makes the news
which makes the views
of those that refuse to see wrong from right

in the UK innocence is sold as **white**
or should I say
it started in the UK
then the **British empire** spread it worldwide
so, **these people** take sides
they think with their eyes
"it must be the **brown** or **black** lad"
then comes all the **mindless backlash**
"clearly the **black** kid overacted"
these mindsets are so **f'in backwards**
never let the truth get in the way of good old **racial bias**
it turns them into **compulsive liars**
doing the government's job for them
perpetuating an "**us against them**"
which has been going on since Lord knows when
and **these people** still don't get the gist
if intelligence is a clear mind
then their mind is mist
a coward dies a thousand deaths
they make bad decisions like a poor ref
with VAR
these people will say "it's a goal"
when it clearly hit the bar
sounding like they've clearly hit the bar
as that went straight over their head
these brains are dead
these people say they love **this country**

but they **hate** "**others**" that love this country
they **hate people** that come to this country
with love for this country
they **hate people** that come from this country
if they don't resemble thee physically
how dare anyone else be successful and comfy
how dare refugees be put in hotels in this country
why are you blaming innocent **people** you numpties
it makes **these people** get all jumpy
especially if **others** have a **different** point of view
especially if **others** have a **different point of hue**
nevertheless, I must stress
Thank God not every **"English" person** is like this
but I've noticed in **my generation** there is an
uncanny likeness
in **these people**
that don't believe in everyone being treated equal
these people are the self-righteous
the **huge minority**
that believe in the book of **whiteness**
I have heard this all my life
to them I am Brit
ish
but not quite
many have made it very clear it's theirs and not mine
and I "**can't be English cus I'm not white**"
like **white** is a birth right

2 Outspoken

I know it's not right
but neither are they
it's gone from **blatant to latent**
when I was a child in my parents' day
the **hate** was rife
I remember being spat in the face by a grown **man**
when I was five
as I write this, I have tears coming out of my eyes
the guy told me to **fuck off back to where I came from**
so scared I got on my bike
my face i wiped
then i rode and cried
back up the road to where I came from
that was my first lesson, and it was painful
my mum taught me the word distasteful
describing **these people**
it was vicious in your face; it was evil
it was live
and many of **these people thrived**
and are still alive
at the expense of **other people**'s lives
a lack of common love, historical knowledge or sense
just contempt
hence nowadays
these people put in their fifty pence
in the **comment haters** section

as they are no longer centre of attention
fragility feels the need to mention their tension
as they "**can't say it in public anymore**"
so**, these people** can't take it anymore
so, anytime they can, they take the floor
and their rhetoric is so easy to predict
like they are reading from a script
different toilet, same shit
you know what's coming next
change makes **these people** vexed
these people think they are getting less
when Britain is getting blessed
from the colonial days of plunder
taken from an array of cultures,
a myriad of flavours
savoured at favourite restaurants and takeaways
sometimes I wish they could take away
all the resources sourced from abroad
with a sign saying be careful what you wish for
most of **these people** would be eating cardboard
listening to the wireless sat on hard boards
you don't know what you got till it's gone
hate stops us being one
hate consumes the vessel that holds it
if morality was a card game **these people** folded
these people have lost the ability
to think critically

they don't think
typically
these people aim angst in the wrong place
"a mind is a terrible thing to waste"
many minds are deteriorating at pace
cus **these people** are consumed with **hate**.

MUSIC

At school i averaged a C/D
at home i got a masters in CDs
listening to music is where you'd see me
every Sunday Dad played vinyl
such a shame they made it final for the vinyl
those days were tribal
sat round listening to records play
all day
i was told *it's my house* by Diana Ross
i never asked when will I be *famous* like Bros
James Brown *paid the cost to be the boss*
ZZ Top
give me all your loving
for music i was buzzing
Lord Kitchener loved the *Sugar Bum Bum* of *Audrey*
i was young but i loved how music told and sold stories
Smokey Robinson showed me the *tears of a clown*
Pagliacci's smile *wore a frown*
cus his wife cheated and left town
in autumn it was *golden brown*
with the Stranglers

the days when i wore my stone washed wranglers
those days were fun
Dad sang *Be my Little Baby* to my mum
Karen Carpenter told me *it's only just begun*
i heard
girls just Wanna have fun with
Cyndi Lauper
Ray Charles had *Georgia*
on his mind
playing music never stopped him from being blind
in that sentence there is a pun inside
as he was one of a kind
such talent is hard to find
nowadays
i suppose that what every generation says
anyway
by 1983 i got to Level 42 *living it up*
till the sun goes down
then Billy Joel told me about this girl *uptown*
i remember when Flash was the Grandmaster
i stepped into a world
when Blondie had me in *raptures*
It captivated and animated my mind
when it's not *playing tricks*
on mine
like Scarface and Bushwick
i would rotate six

or seven different songs at a time
listening to the formation of rhymes
back at mine
sipping some house *red, red wine*
cus i was on the UB40
at college i was naughty
by nature
not cus i hate ya
I just love music like Eric Sermon
of that I was certain
so now I'm reeling in the years like Steely Dan
thinking back to when Nas said, 'You're da **man**'
up till this day I'm still a fan
in the 80s i wore my afro midrange and neat
listening to afro beats
before it took to these streets
before it was called afro beats
The Oriental Brothers, Fela Kuti
Uncle Arinze on blast with me on record duty
teaching us many Igbo words
our traditional music took me to another world
but you could count my collection on two hands
until i was introduced to new bands
my world changed when i first heard Wu Tang
in their *36 chambers of death*
which put me on to Meth
and Mary J Blige

you're all i need to get by
Marvin Gaye and Tammy Terrel did it live
excuse me while I kiss the sky
imagine if Jimi Hendrix was still alive
he was one of a kind
back in the day i listened to Ahmed
can't forget *Amen Amen*
oui senior
blasting out through the pioneers when we got through the door
when we resided in Mickleover
before we moved to Littleover
and a little over a few years later
i put pen to paper
and here we are
i like driving in my car
on some Madness
nostalgia fills my heart with gladness
when i wore *baggy trousers*
around the same time
inspector gadget said wowsers
i remember the cheesy theme tune for Dougie Howser
even though it's cringe
music has that thing
that can take you from winter to spring
take you back to a time
a night

a life
without music life is useless
the buzz of that tune that makes you lose it
so let me get back to the music ay
sitting on the dock of the bay
with Otis Reading
just wasting time till about 7
i *let the music play*
like Shannon did
you can't touch this the way Hammer did
the sweetest taboo with Shola Ama and Glamour kid
oooh ooh
that's the sound of the Police
ooh ooh
that's the sounds of the beats
from krs1 i used to listen to
i remember sitting through
tapes back-to-back
so often the tapes would snap
or get chewed in the cassette player
which my pops worshipped like a prayer
i just hope *papa don't preach*
and i'm not in *trouble deep*
turn up Madonna
if *we're all going on a*
summer holiday
Cliff Richard told us *she's all mine*

the song that inspired my parents to call each other mine
all the time
i heard the Whispers as *the Beat goes on*
with music i was never *lonely* like Akon
no Tears for fears i'd *shout, shout, let it all out*
cus music is the thing that *i can't do without*
come on
i'm talking to you
with a memory or two
good music made me love good lyrics and could recite
a few
most of my poets rapped
J Cole, Kano, Biggie, Jay-Z, Andre 3000, Nas
they were the Shakespeares in my class
to me, lyrically not many can surpass
new music took me on new paths
spiritually
i was in an Oasis
with an eclectic playlist
Definitely Maybe
it's gonna be the one that saves me
for after all
music is my one and all.

THAT *STARE*

That **stare** that you can't compare
any time any place anywhere
you can never prepare
for that **stare**
that says "what **you** doing here?"
that **stare** concocted of **anger** and fear
that **stare** that says **"stay over there"**
that **stare** makes them trip over stairs
that **stare** is fixated
never felt so **hated**
from that **stare**
stooped in a **white legacy of lies**
I realise their real eyes haven't realised
that I know that **stare**
I feel that **stare** all the way from over there
behind that **stare**
humanity no longer lives there
so I **stare** without a care for them or their **stare**
and they quickly snap out of that trance
their pupil's dance
as they avert those **prejudiced** eyes

that were just embedded into my head and torso
like they are gods and I'm a mere mortal
but they don't know I'm fearless like the Kaduna bull
so I stare
and then they look uncomfortable
and I'm suddenly more comfortable
in their discomfort
I respect comfort so I never diss comfort
I miss comfort
when I see that **stare**
I've learned to reciprocate
and stare right back into their face
so, they know I know it's not their place
to **stare** at me anyway
I climb into their heads like a staircase
stay as long as I want then vacate
like a good lawyer I rest my case.

2 OUTSPOKEN

I must be too outspoken
in a country where home truths are too unspoken
where truth speakers are "cancelled"
deemed controversial tokens
which is why i'm open
to debate
in this day and age
I write these words on this page
enraged by the lies we face
day after day
to keep us in categorised cages
trapped in overpriced mortgages
and underpaid wages
by those that pose to be
for us supposedly
are blatantly faking
and known to be
rolling in it like pigs in muck
bringing home the bacon
stuffing their faces
then telling us to work more jobs

to up your wages
how's about up our wages
condescending piss takers
I feel like slapping faces
you don't have to be smart
to see these politicians are just mc's
giving it large
it's all hype when they are on the mic
they just bite bars and recite
they need ghostwriters
to sound nice
telling us sweet little lies
then don't do shite
we have rights
so I'm using mine right
and so should you
be instrumental in using your voice
to eradicate this noise
and on that note, I'm not going to vote
if all I've got is a shit choice
with a posh voice
tell me what's the point
unless we challenge them as one big herd
the **people** don't get heard
choices are made first
for us
we get nothing but words like a thesaurus

trying to pass off as democracy
is demo crazy in the house of cards
the house always wins
unless we go all in
which is why I'm exposing this by speaking out
like an art they've got it down
different anchor same sound
Britain is not the same now
and it's not supposed to be
I'm too outspoken and i'm supposed to be
I can't stay quiet when injustice is always poking me
so i'm goading we
as we are totally engulfed by the abnormal
gambling ads on every minute of the day is "normal"
but gambling for money at a house is unlawful
their hypocrisy is awful
that's why they get a despondent me
when they use slogans like gamble responsibly
are they f#%king kidding me
this is just another systemic hypocritical example
and I don't even gamble
it always boils down to money and power
every second every minute every hour
we are devoured
by the powers that be
making millions of us who struggle
so, millionaires can live comfortably

in a bubble
families struggle to make ends meet
a toss-up between light or heat
getting patronised by the elites
that teach rules they don't adhere to
I believe you
when I see you and hear you
while civilians were locked down and fearful
we were conned by the cons
having a party all merry and cheerful
taking the piss getting pissed
while we were getting stiffed
by that blond prick and his cronies
now there's a new old party back in town
just another political hand to milk the cow
to serve the ubiquitous enemy on a plate
on a daily basis
the sad thing is the spoon-fed love to taste it
it's like they serve **hate** on plates for the tasteless to
taste and rate
like ready steady **hate**
and then they get a taste for it
but the very thing they **hate**,
they eat and become it
for this mindset I just don't have the stomach
my take is
if you portray to be better

then you must be better
you must lead better
instead of using simple minds as bait
the brain has been replaced
by whatever mantra they spray
so how can I stay silent
when I see the misdirected **anger** and violence?
stirred up by the worst lot
that have the ladle to stir pots
as the truth is too hot
so **simple minds** lose the plot
and point their finger at "**you lot**"
which is the definition of pointless
I suggest they point less and learn more
I've seen more critical thinking in year four
equality for all is what I'm here for
so to conclude I must allude to you dudes
that sit on the fence
hence
picking splinters out your bum
imagine if it was your sibling father or mum
how would you feel if you were split from yours?
what if it was you?
what would you do?
you can't tell a person how to walk
If you have never walked in their shoes
when no one speaks up it is a horrible feeling

2 Outspoken

I understand that speaking up may not be appealing
but sometimes we must speak out
the more of us that do the less "odd one out"
the more we look for similarities
the less we see disparities
and I won't have to be **too outspoken**
apparently!!

ABOUT THE MAN HIMSELF

Emeka Ejiofor, the visionary behind the groundbreaking lifestyle brand True Colours Clothing, is a celebrated poet and spoken word artist performing under the moniker True Colours.

He is the author of the critically acclaimed poetry collection Outspoken as well as a professional voiceover artist. As a Trustee of Leicester's Attenborough Arts Centre and a passionate advocate for equality, Emeka champions the ethos of 'Show Your True Colours' (styc), which shines through in his poetry's vibrant celebration of cultural and individual diversity.

A former semi-professional footballer, with experience playing for clubs like Burton Albion, Emeka's multifaceted journey also includes over two decades of inspiring and mentoring young **people** in the education sector. Now an in-demand workshop facilitator, he travels nationwide delivering transformative sytc sessions, earning a powerful reputation for driving meaningful change within the education **system**.

ABOUT TRUE COLOURS

True Colours is centred on self-representation and authenticity, encouraging individuals to embrace cultural and personal differences and express their true selves. As a lifestyle brand, True Colours clothing serves as a medium for the message of show your true colours (sytc), which is the brand's ethos.

Additionally, True Colours incorporates poetry to reinforce themes of equality, shed light on societal issues, and remind us that our commonalities outweigh our differences.

sytc Workshop was created to address significant gaps in traditional education by covering essential topics like racism, mental health, gang involvement, trauma, bullying, sexism, xenophobia and life skills, with a big emphasis on invoking empathy for other people's lived experience.

sytc workshops promote cultural and individual differences, targeting educational and corporate environments to educate about anti-racism and the mental health impacts of racism.

for more information you can find us at
www.sytcworkshop.com

SPECIAL THANKS

I would like to express my deepest gratitude to my family and loved ones as well as everyone who has supported me on this journey, especially those who have bought and endorsed "Outspoken". Your encouragement provided the confidence and motivation I needed to create "2 Outspoken".

A very special thank you to Martin Grey @martingreypoet for his meticulous editing, insightful feedback, and strategic guidance. Your invaluable contributions made this book possible. Your initial edit of the first draft laid the foundation for this work.

Shout out to Conscious Dreams Publishing for all you have done to ensure no stone was unturned in bringing this book to life. I would like to extend my heartfelt thanks to Daniella for her meticulous and dedicated efforts in editing the book, ensuring its polished final form.

Conscious Dreams
PUBLISHING

Transforming diverse writers
into successful published authors

www.consciousdreamspublishing.com

authors@consciousdreamspublishing.com

Let's connect

www.ingramcontent.com/pod-product-compliance
Lightning Source LLC
Chambersburg PA
CBHW061220070526
44584CB00029B/3919